P9-DBO-272

6/15

—LYNNFIELD PUBLIC LIBRARY—
LYNNFIELD, MA 01940

UNTAMED

The Wild Life of
Jane Goodall

ANITA SILVEY

Foreword by Jane Goodall

NATIONAL
GEOGRAPHIC

WASHINGTON, D.C.

LYNNFIELD PUBLIC LIBRARY
18 Summer St.
Lynnfield, MA 01940

Text Copyright © 2015 Anita Silvey
Compilation Copyright © 2015
National Geographic Society

All rights reserved. Reproduction of the whole
or any part of the contents without written
permission from the publisher is prohibited.

Staff for this book

Kate Olesin, Project Editor
Amanda Larsen, Art Director
Hillary Leo, Photo Editor
Marty Ittner, Designer
Carl Mehler, Director of Maps
Paige Towler, Editorial Assistant
Allie Allen and *Sanjida Rashid,* Design Production Assistants
Michael Cassady, Photo Assistant
Erica Holsclaw and *Michael Libonati,* Special
   Projects Assistants
Grace Hill, Associate Managing Editor
Michael O'Connor, Production Editor
Lewis R. Bassford, Production Manager
Robert L. Barr, Manager, Production Services
Susan Borke, Legal and Business Affairs

Published by the National Geographic Society

Gary E. Knell, President and CEO
John M. Fahey, Chairman of the Board
Melina Gerosa Bellows, Chief Education Officer
Declan Moore, Chief Media Officer
Hector Sierra, Senior Vice President and General Manager,
   Book Division

Senior Management Team, Kids Publishing and Media

Nancy Laties Feresten, Senior Vice President; *Jennifer Emmett,* Vice President, Editorial Director, Kids Books; *Julie Vosburgh Agnone,* Vice President, Editorial Operations; *Rachel Buchholz,* Editor and Vice President, *NG Kids* magazine; *Michelle Sullivan,* Vice President, Kids Digital; *Eva Absher-Schantz,* Design Director; *Jay Sumner,* Photo Director; *Hannah August,* Marketing Director; *R. Gary Colbert,* Production Director

Digital

Anne McCormack, Director; *Laura Goertzel, Sara Zeglin,* Producers; *Jed Winer,* Special Projects Assistant; *Emma Rigney,* Creative Producer; *Brian Ford,* Video Producer; *Bianca Bowman,* Assistant Producer; *Natalie Jones,* Senior Product Manager

Special thanks to the Jane Goodall Institute, including
Anna Gibson, Mary Lewis, Jacob Peterson, and Mary Paris,
for contributing their time and effort to this project.

Thanks also to National Geographic Explorer Grace Gobbo
and Dr. David J. Goyder of the Kew Royal Botanic Gardens
for offering their African botanical knowledge.

The National Geographic Society is one of the world's largest nonprofit scientific and educational organizations. Founded in 1888 to "increase and diffuse geographic knowledge," the Society's mission is to inspire people to care about the planet. It reaches more than 400 million people worldwide each month through its official journal, *National Geographic,* and other magazines; National Geographic Channel; television documentaries; music; radio; films; books; DVDs; maps; exhibitions; live events; school publishing programs; interactive media; and merchandise. National Geographic has funded more than 10,000 scientific research, conservation, and exploration projects and supports an education program promoting geographic literacy.

For more information, please visit nationalgeographic.com, call 1-800-NGS LINE (647-5463), or write to the following address:

National Geographic Society
1145 17th Street N.W.
Washington, D.C. 20036-4688 U.S.A.

Visit us online at nationalgeographic.com/books

For librarians and teachers: ngchildrensbooks.org

More for kids from National Geographic:
kids.nationalgeographic.com

For information about special discounts for bulk purchases, please contact National Geographic Books Special Sales: ngspecsales@ngs.org

For rights or permissions inquiries, please contact National Geographic Books Subsidiary Rights: ngbookrights@ngs.org

Library of Congress Cataloging-in-Publication Data

Silvey, Anita, author.

Untamed : the wild life of Jane Goodall / by Anita Silvey.

   pages cm

   ISBN 978-1-4263-1518-3 (hardcover : alk. paper) --
ISBN 978-1-4263-1519-0 (library binding : alk. paper)

1. Goodall, Jane, 1934---Juvenile literature. 2.
Primatologists--England--Biography--Juvenile literature.
3. Women primatologists--England--Biography--Juvenile
literature. 4. Chimpanzees--Behavior--Juvenile literature. 5.
Primatology--Juvenile literature. I. Title. II. Title: Wild life of
Jane Goodall.

   QL31.G58S55 2015

   599.8092--dc23

                        2014017715

Printed in Hong Kong
14/THK/1

National Geographic supports K–12 educators with ELA
Common Core Resources.

Visit natgeoed.org/commoncore for more information.

6-5-15

TABLE OF CONTENTS

(Previous pages) Jane Goodall looks out at Gombe's chimpanzees 35 years after her pioneering research. Now in her 80s, Jane travels more than 300 days per year all over the globe talking to people about conservation. She heads back to Gombe about twice per year to keep up with her beloved chimpanzees.

After years of performing groundbreaking observational chimpanzee research, primatologist Jane Goodall holds hands with a young Figan, who would eventually become alpha male at Gombe.

FOREWORD

Jane Goodall

AS YOU WILL LEARN IN THIS BOOK, I have loved animals all my life. When I was a child, growing up in England, I had various pets, ranging from dogs and cats to guinea pigs and hamsters. But what was most special was being out in nature, watching birds and insects, learning about how they lived their lives.

Because of my passion for learning about animals, I saved up money to buy a ticket to Africa—and was offered the chance to live with and learn about not just any animal but the one most like us, the chimpanzee.

Chimpanzees are more like humans than any other living animal. They have personalities—each one is as different from every other as we are from one another. They have minds that can solve simple problems. They have emotions like happiness and sadness, anger and frustration, and grief. More than 50 years ago, scientists told us that only humans had personalities, thinking minds, and emotions. When I began writing that chimpanzees did too, I was criticized. But I had learned all this long before from my childhood teacher—my dog Rusty!

Now it is known that there is no sharp line separating us from the other animals. Now we know that many other species of animals—including birds and octopuses!—can solve problems. When it comes to feeling pain, science has now proved that fish and lobsters can feel pain. There is so much more to learn.

I hope some of you will want to learn about animals by watching your pets or the wildlife around your home, or, one day perhaps, wolves or bears, lions or kangaroos. And I hope, too, that you will help us protect them. So many animals today are endangered—often because we are destroying the habitats where they live. If we do not work together for conservation, many of these animals will become extinct. And we must not let that happen.

I hope that you will join our Roots & Shoots program for young people. There are groups all over the United States and all over the world. In fact, there is a whole army of young people working to save the natural world, the forests and the prairies, the wetlands and the rivers, the lakes and the oceans. This is important not only for all the animals who call these places home. It is important also for us, and for our own future.

You may feel there is not much you can do to help, but when hundreds and thousands of young people do what they can, it makes a huge difference. So if you love animals, like I do, and if you want to help them, like I do, let us roll up our sleeves together and each do our bit. Remember—your life is important. You make a difference every single day. And you get to choose what sort of difference you want to make.

INTRODUCTION

In recent polls, Jane Goodall has been chosen as the most recognized living scientist in the Western world. She became famous because of her ability to observe and connect with chimpanzees.

As a young girl, Jane studied the behavior of her pets and farm animals. She spent hours waiting for a chicken to lay an egg. She tried to keep earthworms under her pillow. She tempted an ordinary bird into her bedroom as a companion. She trained a dog to do tricks, watching him to understand how his mind worked. But she always wished she could observe animals in more exotic places; in fact, because of the books she read, she wanted to go to Africa.

Then, in her early 20s, she did! And even more amazing things happened after she traveled to a remote area to observe chimpanzees.

This book tells Jane's story, the saga of a girl who loved animals.

Ever since childhood, Jane Goodall dreamed of traveling to Africa and becoming a naturalist. Today, she is a household name because of her discoveries and is a passionate and dedicated advocate for animals and the environment.

Abundant in lower and middle altitudes, this shrub or small tree is widely used in traditional medicine to treat bacterial, fungal, and viral infections, among others. Its flowers can be yellow or red, and it grows small, fleshy berries eaten by both chimps and humans.

Antidesma venosum

This tree grows in wooded grasslands and can reach nearly 98 feet (30 m) high. It can be recognized by its flat, brown, papery-winged pods, which look like large fried eggs. It's highly valued for its termite-resistant wood, which locals use to make furniture and canoes. Its many medicinal uses range from treating ringworm to eye ailments.

Pterocarpus angolensis

Ficus vallis-choudae

A fig tree recognized by its rounded leaves that grow to the size of dinner plates, this plant provides a round, yellow-orange fruit—a very important food for chimpanzees.

Anisophyllea boehmii

This evergreen tree is renowned for its delicious, plum-colored fruit—a sought-after delicacy for both humans and chimps.

Key to Pictured Plants

Plants found in Tanzania's Gombe National Park are important resources for chimps and humans alike. With uses ranging from garden ornamentals to natural medication, Gombe flora are entities of both beauty and utility. While some plants are more prevalent than others, these featured examples are all essential to the thriving ecosystem of Gombe.

Parinari curatellifolia

A medium-size evergreen, this tree has edible fruit and its environmentally friendly timber is useful for rural building projects. Known as *mbula* in western Tanzania, it grows very quickly and can be planted in bulk, without harming or depleting the soil's nutrients. Local people also use its bark as medicine to treat hookworm and malaria.

Scadoxus multiflorus

Also known as the African blood lily, or fireball, this lovely plant yields spherical, softball-size flower heads. Its common name is derived from the bloodlike stains on its white bulbs.

Spathodea campanulata

This large tree is known for its beautiful red-orange flowers, which supply sweet nectar for Gombe's birds. Also called the African tulip tree or Nandi flame tree, people often use it as a decorative tree for yards because of its beauty and shade.

"If you really want something, and you really work hard, and you take advantage of opportunities, and above all if you never give up, you will find a way." —VANNE MORRIS-GOODALL, JANE GOODALL'S MOTHER

CHILDHOOD

Igniting the Fire

Jane Goodall, five years old, had been still for hours, even when the straw had scratched her legs. She couldn't move or make noise. A few feet away, a chicken sat on her nest. Jane had been watching her carefully, observing every move. Then slowly the chicken inched forward. A small round object poked out from the feathers between her legs. After the chicken wiggled, the egg landed on the straw. The chicken clucked, poked the egg with her beak, and strutted. The young girl ran to find her mother and report what had happened!

Young Jane Goodall atop Daniel at Bushel's riding stable in Bournemouth, England, where she first learned to ride horses around 1945.

Jane spends a few moments writing upstairs in her home, surrounded by a now-bald Jubilee, the toy chimp from her childhood, and a photo of her mentor, famed archaeologist Louis Leakey. Today, Jubilee still sits on Jane's dresser in England.

Jane's mother Vanne (pronounced "van") had been searching for her daughter for hours and had become frantic. Now it was almost dark, and Vanne called the police. But then Jane appeared, very excited about her discoveries. At age five, she already understood scientific observation—she had been watching chickens for all those hours to see how they laid eggs. Jane loved all creatures great and small, and she wanted to understand why they acted the way they did.

Valerie Jane Morris-Goodall was born in London on April 3, 1934, but was soon living outside the city. She particularly enjoyed outings with her family to the old Manor House, where her father, Mortimer Morris-Goodall, had grown up. On the grounds stood the ruins of a castle, owned by King Henry II and King Henry VIII. But Jane was fascinated not only by the history of the ruins. She also wanted to learn about the racehorses, cows, and chickens who lived there.

Even Jane's favorite toy was a replica of an animal. When Jane was one year old, her father bought her a large stuffed chimpanzee, Jubilee, made to honor the first chimpanzee born in the London Zoo. Jane took Jubilee everywhere, and the toy chimp became "hairless from all the loving" she gave him as she kept him by her side.

Jane (left) and her sister, Judy (right), with their stuffed animal toys, including Jubilee the chimp. Although Jane's father purchased Jubilee, many stuffed animals of the 1940s were made at home from fabric scraps because of the wartime economy.

When she was about one and a half, Jane found some creatures that fascinated her—earthworms. She even placed them under her pillow. After learning from her mother that they would die without soil, she reluctantly returned the worms to their home in the ground. Once, on a vacation near the sea in Cornwall, England, Jane carried a bucket of seashells from a tide pool. But then Vanne discovered that it contained yellow sea snails, which would die if not in their natural habitat. Jane became hysterical because she realized that she might kill these small creatures. She ran around collecting them so that they could go back to their home.

In fact, Jane could not bear to watch any creature be killed. One day while she sat in a stroller, a dragonfly began to swoop around her. Startled, she screamed. Then someone walking near her stroller hit the dragonfly with a newspaper and then crushed it

As a child, Jane loved all animals, no matter their shape or size, including this pigeon, which she is hand-feeding.

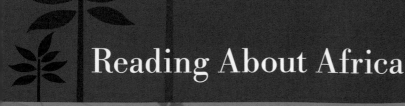

Reading About Africa

Jane first dreamed of going to Africa at age eight, when she read *The Story of Doctor Dolittle* by Hugh Lofting. The kindly doctor traveled to Africa, loved all animals, and kept a menagerie of pets: rabbits in the pantry, white mice in the piano, and a hedgehog in the cellar. His parrot Polynesia taught him to speak and understand animal language, so he was able to become a very successful veterinarian. Years later, Jane traveled to Africa and learned the language of chimpanzees. The Doctor Dolittle books inspired her journey.

Born in England, Hugh Lofting became a world traveler, journeying to Canada, West Africa, and Cuba. While fighting in World War I for the British Army, he wrote stories to his children at home about a kind animal vet, Doctor Dolittle. Later he transformed these tales into *The Story of Doctor Dolittle.*

with his foot. Many years later she wrote, "I can see, with almost unbearable clarity, the glorious shimmering and still quivering wings, the blue 'tail' gleaming in the sunlight, the head crushed on the sidewalk. Because of me it had died."

At any opportunity that she found, she spent time observing animals. One winter, when Jane was sick, a British robin came to her windowsill. She started to put crumbs there every day. It got so tame that it would approach her bed to get the crumbs. Then, in the spring, the robin brought back a mate and made a nest in the bookcase in her bedroom.

In 1939, World War II broke out in Europe. Jane's father, who had been a race-car driver, went to fight the Germans in France. So Jane, her younger sister, Judy, and Vanne moved to Vanne's childhood home, the Birches, in Bournemouth, England. There, Jane explored the sandstone cliffs and long sandy beaches. But despite the beauty of the world around the Birches, she and every other member of the family had a personal gas mask, in case of an attack on England. Their packed suitcases sat by the door, ready if they had to evacuate their home. When air-raid sirens sounded in the night, as German planes flew overhead, the family had to leave their beds and go to their small bomb shelter.

Bournemouth wasn't a main target for German bombers, who were headed for more populated areas like London. But sometimes when the planes returned to Germany, they dropped bombs in the area. One summer day while Vanne, Jane, and Judy were enjoying an outing to the beach, they had a narrow escape.

Jane with her sister, Judy, her mother, Vanne, and her father, Mortimer. Like many men in the 1940s, Mortimer enlisted in the army to help defend England during World War II.

This poster, produced for British Railways, shows a panoramic landscape view of Bournemouth's coast, where Jane and her family lived during the war. Along the cliffs grew pine, oak, and birch trees and Spanish chestnuts. Jane would sometimes harvest and roast the chestnuts over the fire in her sitting room.

They were walking over the sand dunes when suddenly they heard a plane very near to them. Vanne shouted for the girls to lie down in the sand and used her own body to protect them. One of the bombs hit a spot exactly where the family would have been standing on a lane if they had continued on their path home.

Jane was 11 when World War II ended. Even after that time, she rarely saw her father, who had joined a British Army unit in India. He occasionally came back while on leave, but would quickly head out on missions to places like Burma or Hong Kong. In 1950, this absent husband and father asked Vanne for a divorce. So the family stayed at the Birches, where Jane spent the rest of her childhood. In the lovely, redbrick Victorian house, Jane became an avid reader and particularly enjoyed Kipling's *Jungle Book* and Edgar Rice Burroughs's Tarzan books, both set in Africa. The heroine of the Tarzan books happened to be named Jane. Living in a supportive, mostly female

Young Jane with her pet cat at her family home, the Birches, in Bournemouth, England. Jane lived at the Birches with her mother's two sisters, her uncle, two single women left homeless from the war, and Jane's grandmother, known as "Danny" because Jane could not pronounce "Granny" when she was young.

environment at home had certain advantages; as she said later, "I was never, ever told I couldn't do something because I was a girl."

At the Birches, Jane acquired a menagerie of pets. Her tortoise, Johnny Walker, kept disappearing, so they painted his shell red so that he could be found more easily. She cared for caterpillars (lime hawk-moth), a slow worm called Solomon, guinea pigs, cats, a terrapin named Terrapin, and Peter the Canary. A dog named Rusty became her mentor in terms of the animal world. He helped shape Jane's attitude toward animals—and science.

While living at the Birches, Jane attended, as a day student, an all-girls boarding school just a bus ride away. Although she enjoyed time at school with friends, in her diary she often called school "dreary" and all "routine and dullness." She hated to be "stuffed with 'education' from day's dawn to day's eve." She simply wanted to get out of the classroom and into the natural world.

Jane's Favorite Dog

A black dog with a white blaze on his chest, Rusty lived at a hotel that stood next to Jane's house. Every morning, as soon as Rusty was let out, he ran over to see his friend. When let into the house, he bounded up to her bedroom to begin their day of activity.

Soon Jane discovered that Rusty loved to learn tricks—and when she put a dog biscuit on his nose, he tossed it in the air before grabbing the treat. Rusty even enjoyed being placed in a wheelbarrow and moved around; he let Jane dress him up in clothes. But most important, he taught her that animals could reason. When Jane threw a ball out her window, Rusty would watch where it landed, bark to be let out, and then locate it immediately. She realized that he could remember objects that had disappeared.

This photo of Jane and Rusty was taken in Bournemouth in 1954, when Jane was about 20 years old. A note on the back reads, "Jane and Rusty the Inseperables [sic]." Jane later said that Rusty was the one who first taught her that animals have real emotions, personalities, and intelligence.

The Alligator Club

Jane discovered that she not only liked to read about animals but that she also wanted to share her enthusiasm with her friends. At age 12, she organized a nature club, the Alligator Club. Each of the four members, who included Jane's sister, chose their club names after animals. Jane chose the beautiful red admiral butterfly. The members would all line up—Jane first as Red Admiral and then Sally (Puffin), Sue (Ladybird), and Judy (Trout)—to create an alligator formation. They organized secret midnight feasts, raised money to take care of old horses, and created a museum of their natural treasures like seashells and feathers. Jane drew up the rules for earning badges. In short, she created her own scout troop, which produced a magazine called the *Alligator Letters*, for which she wrote articles, quizzes, and puzzles.

(From top to bottom) Jane with Rusty and fellow members of the Alligator Club: Sally Cary, Sue Cary, and Judy Goodall. As part of the club, the girls turned the glass conservatory, or greenhouse, into a museum and asked visitors to drop coins in the collection box. Money raised by the Alligator Club was donated to rescue old horses.

After graduating from high school, Jane didn't really know what she wanted to do for work. In fact, she found the idea of "earning a living ... almost frightening," though she considered becoming a journalist or writer. Vanne convinced Jane to attend secretarial school so that her daughter could learn typing and bookkeeping and find steady employment.

After becoming trained as a secretary, Jane went to work in the filing department at the Registrar's Office at Oxford University, a job she found exceedingly dull. Her supervisor did allow Jane to bring her pet hamster, Hamlette, to work, but otherwise the "boredom of this foul job" seemed terrible to her. At lunchtime she loved canoeing on the River Cherwell, where she could glimpse moorhens, kingfishers, and swans. But then she had to go back into an office—and file.

To help Jane, a friend of the family set up an interview for her at a commercial film studio in London, Stanley Schofield Productions. Jane enjoyed her daily tasks at the film studio—editing film and finding background music. But office jobs and living in the city took her very far away from the natural world.

Then she received a letter that contained an amazing invitation.

While in school, Jane had developed a friendship with Marie-Claude (Clo) Mange, whose father acquired a farm in Africa, outside Nairobi, in Kenya. Clo invited Jane to come stay for six months with her on the farm. The note ignited Jane's old desire to see Africa. She quit her London job, headed back to the Birches, where she could live cheaply, and began waitressing at a hotel to earn money for the trip. A lackluster secretary, Jane became a brilliant waitress and could carry up to 13 plates without a tray! After four months of nonstop work, she managed to earn enough money for passage to Kenya.

Finally, Jane was going to do something that she'd always wanted to do. She had dreamed about Africa during her childhood. Wild animals. Adventures. Untamed land. She could not believe her good fortune. Now she was setting out to see it all.

Living at Bournemouth

Though Jane lived at Bournemouth year-round, her family and close friends spent a few weeks vacationing at the beach for a couple of summers. During World War II, Bournemouth's long beach was barricaded against attack, so the family didn't play there. But Vanne brought the girls to a more secluded cove called Studland, farther up the coast from Bournemouth. Vanne rented a cottage there and Jane, Judy, and close friends Sue and Sally played on the beach and visited the farm animals that lived nearby.

Jane called her childhood "idyllic," and she later wrote that her experiences growing up near Bournemouth's tall cliffs and sandy shores became the foundation for her love of the natural world.

DURLEY CHINE

BOURNEMOUTH BAY

SAN REMO HOTEL
DURLEY ROAD
BOURNEMOUTH.

THE

Jane's favorite dog, Rusty, actually lived in the San Remo Hotel and came to visit Jane's house each morning.

Resort Town

This postcard showcases the highlights of Bournemouth, such as the San Remo Hotel and beaches. Bournemouth was founded as a seaside resort town in the mid-1880s and remains a popular vacation destination for more than five million visitors every year.

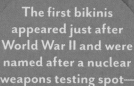

The first bikinis appeared just after World War II and were named after a nuclear weapons testing spot—Bikini Atoll.

War Zone

A woman sunbathes during a wartime bank holiday surrounded by barbed wire on the beach at Bournemouth in August 1944. While Bournemouth escaped most of the wartime bombings, the beach was lined with minefields and barbed wire barriers. Huge guns were also placed on top of the cliffs for protection.

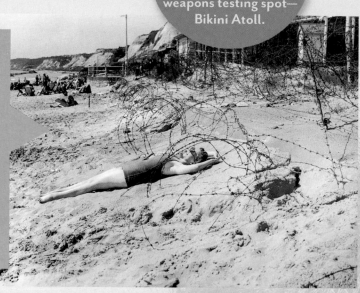

White Cliffs

Bournemouth is a short distance from England's Jurassic Coast, which harbors Triassic, Jurassic, and Cretaceous cliffs from the Mesozoic era. These cliffs display about 185 million years of Earth's history, and the area is now a World Heritage site.

Bournemouth is well known for its cliffs called chines—deep, narrow ravines that have been cut through soft rocks by water descending to the sea.

"One of the males [chimpanzees] stood upright to watch more closely ... He must have weighed a good 130 pounds [59 kg] ... Later I was to learn how it feels to be slammed on the head from behind by a large male chimpanzee, but fortunately for me he did not continue his attack." —JANE GOODALL

GOMBE

Hunting and Gathering

On March 13, 1957, Jane Goodall embarked on her journey to Africa, traveling on the ship *Kenya Castle*. When she finally arrived at her friend Clo's farm, the family celebrated with a cake for Jane's 23rd birthday. "Right from the moment I got here I felt at home," Jane wrote to her family.

But if Jane wanted to stay in Africa, she needed to find a job. One of her friends suggested that since she was interested in animals, she should visit Louis Leakey, the head of Coryndon Museum (later called the National Museum of Kenya). When they met,

Jane climbs a tree in Gombe, binoculars in hand, to better view chimpanzees. Jane was used to climbing trees; as a child, she used to sit in them for hours and read.

he talked nonstop about snakes and lungfish. Jane was enthralled. She loved his untidy office filled with bones, teeth, Stone Age tools; it even included a big cage with a pygmy mouse and six babies. Impressed by Jane's knowledge of wildlife, Leakey hired her as his secretary.

It was a life-changing job for Jane Goodall.

Working with Leakey fascinated Jane, but it soon became clear that he had other plans for her. His research on the ancestors of man led him to believe that large apes should be studied in the wild. Leakey believed that any behaviors modern humans and apes shared might help scientists understand how the first human beings acted. Studying chimps in the wild would be dangerous and would require a person physically strong and willing to spend long months away from civilization. Leakey had been hunting for the ideal candidate, preferably someone with a mind "uncluttered by theories." He kept talking to his new secretary about this idea, and Jane found it absolutely breathtaking. In Louis Leakey, Jane found a mentor who had plans and dreams far greater than working in a museum.

One day, when Leakey was speaking about the need to study the great apes, Jane blurted out, "Louis, I wish you wouldn't keep talking about it, because that's just what I want to do."

"I've been waiting for you to tell me that," he replied.

Three chimps sit in lush forest trees at the Chimpanzee Rehabilitation Trust's Badi Mayo camp in Gambia, in Africa. Chimps currently inhabit 21 African countries and are most often found in the rain forests.

Louis Leakey, Jane's Mentor

Louis Leakey had experienced the kind of childhood Jane had dreamed of while growing up in England. The son of British missionary parents, he was raised in Kenya and once kept a baboon as a pet. After going to Cambridge University to secure his doctorate, he returned to Africa to dig for fossils and to help prove Charles Darwin's hypothesis that the human race originated in Africa. In the years after meeting Jane, Leakey became famous because of his work in the Olduvai Gorge, where he discovered some of the first ancestors of human beings.

Louis Leakey was a famed paleontologist, archaeologist, and anthropologist who studied the origin of humans. Here he demonstrates how to skin a ram with Stone Age tools.

Vanne Morris-Goodall, Jane's Mother

Described by those who met her as an impressive lady with true grit, Vanne Morris-Goodall immediately became essential to Jane in Gombe. Because Vanne stayed in the camp rather than heading out to do fieldwork, she set up a local clinic, dispensing medicines and taking care of wounds. Louis Leakey had assured Vanne that the best way to make friends in this area was to provide medical help, and she had come prepared with the supplies needed. Shortly after setting up the clinic, Vanne had a line of people who needed her help. One Bantu mother carried her son six miles (10 km) to visit the camp clinic.

Jane Goodall and her mother, Vanne, sort specimens in her tent at Gombe Stream Game Reserve, now Gombe National Park.

With Jane on board, Leakey hunted for funding and secured the appropriate permits for her to work in the Gombe Stream Game Reserve in Tanganyika (now Gombe National Park in Tanzania). She then faced one last hurdle from officials, who objected to the idea of a young woman traveling by herself into this remote area. Jane's mother, Vanne, volunteered to go to Gombe with Jane for a few months, until they had established a camp and reassured the officials.

On Thursday, July 14, 1960, Jane Goodall, 4,000 miles (6,437 km) away from home, set off for Gombe Stream Game Reserve's 60 square miles (155 sq km) of rugged country. Jane had one goal: to find the region's elusive chimpanzees and to observe them for as long as she could. Unarmed and untrained, she ventured into this strange new world. No one had ever observed wild chimpanzees for more than two months.

Jane would eventually study three generations of chimpanzees over a 55-year period, one of the longest continuous field studies of wild animals ever conducted. She loved the spot instantly: "It is so beautiful, with the crystal clear blue lake, the tiny white pebbles on the beach, the sparkling ice cold mountain stream, the palm nut trees, the comical baboons ... It is the Africa of my childhood's dreams, and I have the chance of finding out things which no one has ever known before."

Upon their arrival at Gombe, Jane and Vanne, with the help of a game ranger, two guides, and their cook, Dominic, set up a tent close to the beach. It had a separate washroom in the back, a porch in the front, and small windows covered with mosquito netting. A bubbling stream tumbled down behind the tent. They dug a hole in the ground, surrounded by woven palm leaves, that would serve as their latrine. For some, the accommodations might have seemed daunting or primitive. Jane felt she had arrived in paradise: Being in the wild, away from people, close to animals, seemed like heaven to her.

Gombe included a veritable Noah's ark of animals—buffalo, bush pigs, hippos, pythons, crocodiles, leopards, and smaller creatures such as mongooses and elephant

shrews. Although Jane enjoyed watching all of them, she was eager to get close to the chimps and observe what they did every day. But they instinctively ran away from her—a strange white and hairless primate intruding into their territory.

Eventually, with barely adequate field binoculars, Jane was able to watch them forage for fruit and stuff themselves with berries. One chimp, reclined against a branch and propped up on one elbow, picked fruit with one hand. Jane tasted all the foods the chimps ate, and she discovered where they slept—in nests

Young researcher Jane Goodall outside her tent at Gombe Stream Game Reserve. Although British authorities at the time did not want a young woman traveling in the jungle by herself, Jane loved being in the wilderness and did everything she could to extend her time there.

constructed in trees. After finding a horizontal fork in a tree, the chimps pulled together several branches. When Jane climbed up to test one of the nests, she found the sleeping spots comfortable and springy.

Although Jane had no survival training, she had the right constitution for living in the wilderness. She could go for hours without food and water and was a master at patiently watching what occurred around her. To get more observation time during the day, she would sleep outside at night near where the chimps had made a nest.

Although Jane always downplayed the difficulties of her task, she faced all kinds of problems and obstacles. Following chimpanzees as they moved through the forest was a huge challenge. Because of the thick, dense undergrowth, she often had to crawl through it or wiggle over the ground on her stomach. She continuously removed thorns from her hair, skin, and clothes. As she moved, her shoes got caught in vines, and as she tried to pull free, she often saw the black shapes of the chimps vanishing.

Jane and chimp Fifi observe each other in Gombe. During the beginning of Jane's research, she was often frustrated that she could not get near the chimpanzees without scaring them away. However, over time, they grew used to her presence, and she was able to get closer to them.

Jane's African Pets

Not surprisingly, one of the first things Jane did in Africa was acquire pets, often more unusual than the ones she had been able to keep in England. She found a bush baby, a small squirrel-size primate who made a wailing sound at night and sounded like a baby crying, who she named Levi. Soon Levi was leaping from various spots, playing hiding games, and sleeping under Jane's blouse. She also acquired a mongoose named Kip and a vervet monkey called Kombo, who were attracted to each other and cuddled together. A pet mongoose wasn't such an exotic thing to Jane, who had read Rudyard Kipling's *Jungle Book* as a child, with its famous fictional mongoose, Rikki-Tikki-Tavi.

A bush baby clings to a tree. Large eyes and oversize ears help the animal track insect prey at night.

While searching for chimps, Jane traveled over an unmapped, unknown terrain filled with unexpected cliffs and valleys. In some places, a wrong step could be dangerous. Years later, a Gombe researcher fell down a cliff while following chimpanzees and died. Jane herself had crossed this terrain many times—but had avoided injury.

Some of her difficulties were relentless, like the tsetse flies, fast-moving gray insects with a painful bite. They feasted on people in the wilderness.

Some of her obstacles were fierce. Once, when Jane was sitting at her favorite observation point, she heard a strange mewing. Then about 15 yards (14 m) away she saw a leopard approaching; she could just glimpse the white tip of his tail above the grass. The leopard was headed directly toward her! Silently, she moved away from this dangerous predator, to make sure he didn't attack her. Jane, rarely frightened of anything, had "an ingrained illogical fear" of leopards. When she came back later to her perch, she found his scat right on the spot she had been sitting—left there so that his scent would mask that of

Chimpanzees have many ways of communicating with each other over short or long distances. One of these calls is known as the "pant-hoot," which is unique to each chimpanzee.

the alien creature who had moved into his territory.

As she searched tirelessly for the chimps throughout the day, Jane did everything she could think of to make them less afraid of her. She dressed in drab greens and browns so that she fit in with the foliage. Soon realizing that the chimps did not like to be looked at, she would glance away from them when near, pretending to be uninterested. And when she noticed that a chimp was gazing at her, she would act just like another primate and dig in the ground as if hunting for insects to eat.

At first, Jane felt frustrated because she could not get close enough to the chimps for her own satisfaction. However, being near these large, wild animals could be quite dangerous. One time, during a rainstorm, Jane suddenly saw a chimp hunched on the ground in front of her. Then overhead she saw another, who gave a loud, spine-chilling call. Other chimps around her began to shake branches and call. Jane sat down, trying to appear nonthreatening. One of the chimps charged at her, hair bristled. But at the last minute, he veered off. Two more chimps charged. Then, suddenly, they all disappeared. Jane desperately wanted to make contact with and be accepted by the chimps. Over time, they lost their fear of her.

Jane had to not only find ways to get close to the chimps but also stay healthy enough to do so. The unfamiliar food, water, and living conditions could easily lead to serious illness. At one point, both Jane and Vanne succumbed to some kind of fever, probably malaria. They registered temperatures of 104° and 105°F (40° and 40.6°C) and lay on cots next to each other. Throbbing headaches and weakness plagued them for three weeks. Vanne nearly died. Despite her slow recovery, Jane insisted on hunting for chimps, although she found climbing to her observation point exhausting.

After weeks of relatively unproductive observation, Jane met the chimp who would make her scientific breakthroughs at Gombe possible. She named him David Greybeard. A handsome male with a white beard, he was obviously an older member of the chimp community. He came within 10 yards (9 m) of Jane. He stared at her, amazed. Then he cocked his head from one side to the other and scampered off into the undergrowth. Climbing up into a small tree, David peered down at Jane again, fascinated with this new white animal.

David Greybeard

Without David Greybeard, Jane might have had to abandon her fieldwork before she was able to get close enough to the chimpanzees to make critical observations. He was the first chimpanzee she saw eating meat and the first she saw using tools. He also was the first chimp to take a banana from her hands. He seemed less bothered by her than the other chimps did. Because he accepted Jane as just another primate, the other animals became less wary of her.

David Greybeard eats some bananas outside Jane Goodall's tent. The bananas helped lure the chimps out from the forest. David loved the fruit and once ate 50 bananas in one sitting.

Since David did not seem to fear Jane, he let her get closer to him than the other chimps permitted. One day, Jane heard chimps making angry screams and went to see what was happening. David held a pink object, which Jane thought might be a newborn infant. Instead, she realized that the chimps were eating the object, sucking on it. They had killed an infant bush pig and made a meal of it. Until this observation, everyone had assumed that chimpanzees ate only plants, nuts, and fruits. Now Jane had recorded a clear incident of meat-eating. And a week later, she saw something even more amazing.

Setting out to follow some cries and hoots, Jane observed a chimp sitting in front of a termite mound. As she got closer, she realized that the chimp, David Greybeard, had broken off a long grass stalk, about 18 inches (48 cm) in length, and put it in the mound to capture some plump winged termites. The soldier termites, annoyed by the intrusion into their nest, clamped their jaws on the grass stalk. Then David pulled the stalk out of the mound and ate the termites on it. Later she observed other chimps engaged in termite "fishing."

Jane had never "dreamed of seeing anything so exciting." Even more thrilling, she watched David Greybeard and his friend Goliath pick up small twigs and strip off the leaves. They modified an object to make a tool—a behavior that was believed by scientists to be unique to humans.

Every week Jane wrote to Louis Leakey to describe what she had seen and her progress. At this point, scientists defined human beings as "man, the toolmaker." But when Leakey received her report of the chimps' making and using tools, he responded to her breakthrough with a telegram: "Now we must redefine 'tool,' redefine 'man,' or accept chimpanzees as human."

At age 26, alone and unaided in the wilderness, Jane Goodall had changed the way scientists defined both humans and chimpanzees.

No. 1.

During her research at Gombe (right), Jane found that chimpanzees are tool-using, intelligent, and emotional beings with a complex social structure. Like humans, they feel love, hate, fear, and joy in their daily dealings with each other. She wrote down her observations in notebooks, like this 1961 entry in a field notebook (below). She recorded observations such as these filmstrip tracings (bottom) of chimp locomotion.

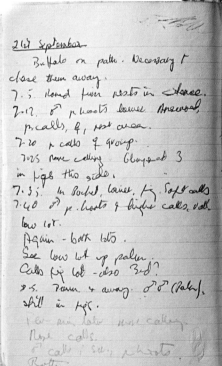

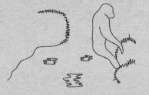

Animals of Gombe

From the moment Jane arrived in Africa, she filled her journals with comments about the creatures that she was encountering for the first time. Some were small and tame enough to keep near her as companions, while others roamed the wild. Although incredibly fearless, Jane admitted that she had an irrational fear of leopards. Otherwise, she delighted in watching baboons, mongooses, and all the other animals that roamed Gombe.

Vervet monkeys live in groups, called troops, of up to 50 individuals.

Vervet Monkeys

Before she came to Gombe, Jane kept a vervet monkey, called Kombo, as a pet. He liked to sleep in her bed and curled up under her blankets.

Mongooses

While in Nairobi, Kenya, Jane had a pet mongoose, Kip, "the sweetest little thing," who would crack open eggs by throwing them at a wall.

Mongooses are omnivores and eat eggs, fruits, nuts, and small prey. Some species are even known to attack cobras.

Baboons

At Gombe, Jane was fascinated by the complex encounters between chimps and baboons. Sometimes baboons, barking loudly, would chase the chimps around.

Unlike many other monkeys, baboons do not have prehensile tails— ones that can grip things.

The word *hippopotamus* comes from an ancient Greek word meaning "river horse."

Hippos

On occasion, Jane would see a hippo, one of the largest animals at Gombe, submerged in the waters of Lake Tanganyika.

Leopards

While Jane was trying to observe chimpanzees, one of the leopards of Gombe came upon her by surprise and even left scat where she had been.

Leopards can live in many different ecosystems, from deserts to mountains and even rain forests.

"It is so beautiful, with the crystal clear blue lake, the tiny white pebbles on the beach, the sparkling ice cold mountain stream, the palm nut trees, the comical baboons."

—JANE GOODALL, WRITING ABOUT GOMBE TO HER FAMILY

CELEBRITY SCIENTIST

The Price and Possibilities of Fame

During Jane's first few months at Gombe, she feared that the project might be called off if she made no progress with the chimpanzees. But after her scientific breakthroughs, Louis Leakey approached the National Geographic Society for funding for Jane's work. At this critical phase, the Society stepped in to help; over the next few years, it would provide no less than 27 grants to keep Jane's study running. Now that Jane had built trust with some of the chimpanzees, she could focus on getting to know their personalities and the details of their complex society.

Jane and a chimpanzee hold up the National Geographic Society flag. Through Louis Leakey, National Geographic knew about Jane's early research and stepped in to fund it.

CHAPTER 3

Unlike traditional scientists who believed that chimps should be identified by numbers, Jane firmly maintained that they must be viewed as distinct beings—with emotions, personalities, and minds capable of solving complex problems. At first, Jane focused on the differing physical characteristics of each chimp. She made scientific notations about them, giving each particular chimpanzee a name that seemed appropriate. Then she began to fill in her understanding by getting to know each chimp's personality.

One of the most easily recognizable of the chimps, old Flo had ragged ears, a bulbous nose, and spindly legs. Flo traveled with two of her children—three-year-old

Flo allows her baby Flint to approach Jane. Flint was the fourth of Flo's five children and the first infant whose progress and development Jane was able to monitor in full.

Goliath

The dominant male of Gombe when Jane arrived was Goliath, who was often in the presence of his best friend, David Greybeard. The two fought alongside each other and played with each other. They particularly liked to tickle each other and then would roar with laughter.

Goliath in Gombe Stream Game Reserve, Tanganyika (known as Tanzania today). Jane often observed David and Goliath using tools to fish termites from their mounds.

Fifi and Figan, who was about eight. Flo impressed Jane as a wonderful mother—affectionate, protective, tolerant, and playful with her charges. Jane felt an incredible kinship with Flo, understanding things about the chimpanzee intuitively that she could not even yet define in scientific terms. Jane herself had a supportive and attentive mother in Vanne. In this chimpanzee community, Jane watched that same type of behavior in Flo.

Jane determined that Flo was the dominant female at Gombe. Chimpanzees, like most animals, maintain a hierarchical order, with an alpha male chimp at the top. Although some of the alpha chimps at Gombe won this position by strength and aggression, Jane was able to record variations on this pattern. Mike, the alpha chimp for six years, managed to rise to prominence because of his brains. While visiting Jane's camp, Mike discovered that empty kerosene cans made a terrible noise when rolled along the ground. So Mike began displays of hitting the cans and kicking them before the other high-ranking males. He completely intimidated them with his newfound strategy.

Louis Leakey arranged for Jane to attend Cambridge University, in England, where he had also studied.

Jane was fascinated not only by individuals but also by group behavior. One day, as it began to rain, she saw a large group of chimps. But rather than seeking shelter, one or two of them emerged into the open, staring at Jane. Then they organized themselves into two distinct groups and began climbing up a hill in the pelting rain. One of the males, who Jane called Paleface, reached the top of the hill, swiped at a bush, and then began to charge down the hill. He broke off a branch, kept it in his hand, and then reached a tree at the bottom and climbed up into it. The rain was falling very hard now, creating a vague, misty landscape. One chimp after another went through the same ritual. With the continual thunder, lightning, and rain, Jane felt as if she were in a dream. She called the movements of the chimps a "rain dance."

Much would be written later about how Jane's research approach to the chimpanzees seemed more in keeping with the way a woman, rather than a man, might operate. She did not try to master the environment; rather, she observed it. But Jane made all of her discoveries by hard, determined, persistent work. She simply devoted more hours to observation and recording than anyone in the area of chimpanzee research. And she did so through illnesses such as malaria, horrible weather, and rough living conditions.

Jane Goodall spent many hours on a high peak in Gombe Stream Game Reserve, searching through binoculars and a telescope for chimpanzees in the forest below. "The Peak," as she called it, was her favorite observation point.

1 Chimpanzees make and use tools. For a long time, scientists believed that only humans made tools.

2 Chimpanzees hunt and eat small mammals.

3 Chimpanzees also eat fruits, nuts, seeds, blossoms, leaves, and many kinds of insects.

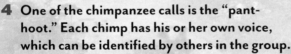

A chimpanzee rests on a liana vine in Gabon (above). A young chimpanzee uses a grass stem to fish for termites in Gombe National Park, Tanzania (left). A female chimpanzee carries her baby on her back (below).

4 One of the chimpanzee calls is the "pant-hoot." Each chimp has his or her own voice, which can be identified by others in the group.

5 Chimpanzees laugh when they play.

6 Chimpanzees groom each other, picking out ticks and burrs. This helps calm nervous chimps and leads to stronger relationships in the chimp community.

7 When chimpanzees are frightened or angry, their hair stands on end.

8 Mothers and the young are always together, up to about age seven.

9 Chimpanzees communicate much like humans—kissing, embracing, patting on the back, touching hands, or tickling.

By the early 1960s, Jane was the foremost scholar in chimpanzee research in the world. Aware of Jane's incredible contributions to the scientific community, Louis Leakey arranged for her to become a Ph.D. candidate at Cambridge University in England. To earn the degree, Jane spent several years dividing her time equally at Cambridge and at Gombe. At Cambridge, she attended seminars, worked with a supervisor, and learned new ways of recording and analyzing scientific data. Although she found some of these approaches helpful, Jane refused

Jane and photographer Hugo van Lawick observe a family of chimpanzees grooming each other in Gombe. On the recommendation of Louis Leakey, Hugo went to Gombe to photograph and film Jane's studies.

to back down from her own intuitive methods of observation. She believed that she understood the animals at Gombe far better than did Cambridge professors who had never lived out in the wild. In 1965, Jane received a doctorate, scientific credibility, and grounding in scientific method. She could then call herself Dr. Jane Goodall.

When Jane started her degree, only a small group of scientists had heard about her work. But then, in the summer of 1961, National Geographic sent a professional photographer, Hugo van Lawick, into Jane's secluded domain to capture her work in Gombe on film. Born in Indonesia and son of a Dutch baron, Hugo moved to Australia and then England as a boy. He found that he loved living close to the natural world and pursued a career in photography. Before coming to Gombe, he was living in Nairobi, Kenya, specializing in images of African animals.

Hugo and Jane had so much in common. Both loved being with wild creatures; both were incredible workers. And Hugo benefited tremendously from all that Jane had accomplished: two of the chimps, David and Goliath, by now had no fear of humans, so Hugo could approach them close enough to take photographs. Jane and Hugo worked together during the day and talked over a campfire at night, a conversation of "chimp—chimp—and more chimp. Hugo loves them as much as I do," Jane wrote home.

In August 1963, Jane's article "My Life Among Wild Chimpanzees," illustrated with Hugo's photographs, appeared in *National Geographic* magazine and was mailed to three million subscribers. The article introduced Jane Goodall and her chimpanzees to the world, and it brought Hugo and Jane together. They were married in 1964, and their wedding cake was decorated with a clay model of David Greybeard. Portraits of the chimps of Gombe greeted guests at the reception.

A year later, just over five years after Jane arrived at Gombe, she became known to millions of Americans. On December 22, 1965, CBS broadcast *Miss Goodall and the Wild Chimpanzees* to 20 million North American viewers. In this documentary, prepared by National Geographic and Hugo, Jane emerges young, vibrant, and courageous. The show conveyed how close she came to the chimps and her determination as she faced the elements with bare arms, legs, and sometimes feet.

August 1963's issue of *National Geographic* magazine, the first time Jane was featured in the publication

Mr. McGregor

Bald on his head, shoulders, and neck, Mr. McGregor loved eggs and often stole them from the camp when he could. He was always a bit belligerent toward Jane and would shake a branch at her if she came too close. She named him after the ornery gardener in Beatrix Potter's *Tale of Peter Rabbit*. Stricken down by the human disease of polio, Mr. McGregor had trouble gathering food, and most of the chimpanzees shunned him, except his regular companion, Humphrey.

Mr. McGregor in the Gombe Stream Game Reserve. Jane believed that his companion, Humphrey, was probably his brother.

The faces of the baby chimps, which looked particularly human, stared out of the television. Both the subject matter and the scientist captivated the imagination of the viewers.

A scientific innovator, an articulate spokesperson with a soft voice, Jane introduced those who had never heard of Gombe to her African setting. Her story even had a romantic ending—with her marriage to Hugo, she became a baroness. From that moment on, Jane would ascend to her position as the most recognized scientist in the Western world. And she was very young to be such a celebrity—only 31 years old.

After the television special, and with her newfound fame, Jane was able to pursue some of her dreams surrounding Gombe. She had always wanted to create a research center there. First, the staff erected prefabricated buildings paid for by National Geographic. But after that, more permanent structures were built, providing some comfort for a growing number of researchers and support staff. Jane spent much of her time at Gombe training researchers so that her work would continue while she was traveling. Because Hugo often took assignments photographing wildlife in various parts of Africa, Jane had to find ways to manage Gombe from afar while with him. Now she

Jane stands in Lawick Lodge at Gombe, watching Melissa the chimpanzee get curious about Jane's baby, Grub. A few years earlier, Melissa had given birth to her own baby, Goblin.

had less time to be in Gombe—or "paradise" as she liked to call it.

Eventually both the paradise of Gombe and Jane, personally, faced challenges. Chimpanzees can contact human diseases, and a polio epidemic broke out among her beloved apes. Jane's researchers attempted to curb the epidemic by delivering oral polio vaccines in bananas, but several of the chimps became infected. One of Jane's favorite chimpanzees, Mr. McGregor, died of the disease. Jane was devastated by this loss.

In 1967, Hugo and Jane had a son, Hugo Eric Louis, nicknamed Grub. He grew up in the wild, living much of the time in a tent on the Serengeti. Because chimpanzees had been known to attack human infants, Jane and Hugo built a caged veranda onto their house to keep their son safe when he was at Gombe.

During this period of her life, Jane continued writing about her experiences at Gombe. As a child, she had dabbled in being an author and editor with the Alligator Club. Now she was approached to publish books. In the next few decades, Jane created scholarly tomes such as *The Chimpanzees of Gombe;* books for children, including

My Life With the Chimpanzees; and her autobiography, *In the Shadow of Man*, published in 1971. Now in print for more than 40 years, *In the Shadow of Man* provides a highly readable and compelling account of Jane's experiences tracking chimpanzees in the wild. Her memoir brings the chimpanzees who Jane loved so much to life. She wrote about each of them in detail and what she had learned about chimpanzee society. Quickly appearing on the best-seller lists in both the United States and England, the book has since been translated into 48 languages and has never gone out of print. In fact, *In the Shadow of Man* has been one of the most successful books about science ever published.

Jane's success as an author meant more invitations to give lectures around the world, and these demands pulled her away from Gombe for months at a time. Hugo's work as a filmmaker took him to different locations. The two began spending more and more time apart. And when Grub was seven, Hugo and Jane divorced, a painful event in her life.

By now, Jane's research center had been established; local Tanzanians and foreign students spent many hours observing the chimps and compiling scientific data about them. Over the next decades, Jane would have to carve out periods when she could go back to Gombe. But when she returned, she no longer found a place of solitude. Reporters, film crews, and other scientists flocked there to see the work that was taking place.

And so for Jane, her moments of being alone in the forest with chimpanzees—the very thing she had found so much pleasure in—were less and less frequent. Jane had come a long way from being an untrained girl from England, but she had paid a high price to get there.

Jane holds her book *The Chimpanzees of Gombe: Patterns of Behavior*. The 600-plus-page scholarly work is the result of 26 years of observation.

Leakey's Angels

Because Jane Goodall's work was so successful, Louis Leakey found other women to research different great apes around the world. Both Dian Fossey and Biruté Galdikas were selected by Leakey to study primates in their natural environment. Just as he did with Jane Goodall, Leakey secured funding for their continued fieldwork and supported them in their missions.

Dian Fossey spent 18 years in the forests of Rwanda. She wrote *Gorillas in the Mist* about her work with the species.

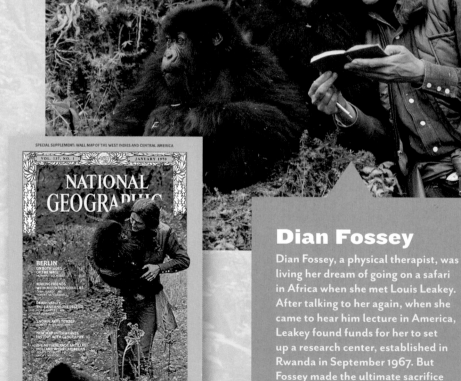

Dian Fossey

Dian Fossey, a physical therapist, was living her dream of going on a safari in Africa when she met Louis Leakey. After talking to her again, when she came to hear him lecture in America, Leakey found funds for her to set up a research center, established in Rwanda in September 1967. But Fossey made the ultimate sacrifice for her work as a scientist—she was murdered while in the field in 1985.

Biruté Galdikas

The youngest of Leakey's protégées, Biruté Galdikas was born in 1946. She and her parents fled Europe after the Soviet occupation of Lithuania and went to live in Ontario, Canada. As a child, she was fascinated with the picture books about Curious George, the monkey.

While working on a doctorate in anthropology at the University of California, Los Angeles, Galdikas met Louis Leakey and told him she would love to study orangutans in the wild. In 1971, Galdikas, with her husband, Rod Brindamour, traveled to Indonesia with help from Leakey and the National Geographic Society. She continues to live there today, studying her beloved orangutans.

Biruté Galdikas was drawn to orangutans because of their beady and adorable eyes.

Leakey called the three researchers the "Trimates." But when Biruté Galdikas wrote her book *Reflections of Eden*, she dubbed them "Leakey's Angels." All three of these women made important scientific discoveries and spent years in the field observing different branches of the ape family. Both Fossey and Galdikas modeled their approach to the animals on techniques that had worked for Jane Goodall.

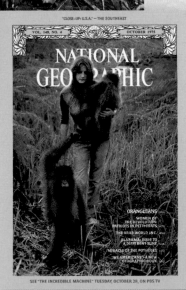

TRANSFORMATION
A Broader Mission

Twenty years after Jane Goodall first appeared on television, a seemingly ordinary event, a scientific conference, changed her direction and her life. From November 7 to 9, 1986, Jane attended an international conference, "Understanding Chimpanzees," sponsored by the Chicago Academy of Sciences in the United States. During the conference, Jane heard stories of chimpanzees being hunted across Africa. She saw photos of chimpanzees imprisoned in tiny cages in medical research labs. She wrote, "When I arrived at Chicago, I was a research scientist ... When I left, I was already, in my heart, committed to conservation and education."

Jane Goodall shows pictures of wild chimpanzees to LaVieille, a chimp who had been kept as a pet most of her life, at the Republic of the Congo's Pointe-Noire Zoo. When the zoo was closed in 1992, LaVieille went to the Jane Goodall Institute's Tchimpounga Chimpanzee Rehabilitation Center, where she became a surrogate mother for its newest arrivals.

CHAPTER 4

A young chimpanzee gazes out through the bars of its cage at the Tchimpounga Chimpanzee Rehabilitation Center (above). Through Jane's efforts, the sanctuary was built to care for orphaned chimps confiscated by the government from traders. Chimpanzee orphans arriving at Tchimpounga are fed fortified milk (below).

During the final hours, those assembled formed an organization that would lobby on behalf of chimpanzees, and Jane agreed to serve as the publicity representative.

"This is no time for doubt or weakness. It is the supreme hour to which we have been called," Winston Churchill stated in a July 4, 1940, message to Americans—a favorite quote of Jane's, which she now put into action. She had gone to Africa because of her love of animals; in the end, her devotion to the chimpanzees of Gombe made her realize that she should fight for their rights and for the rights of all other animals on Earth. For the rest of her life, Jane Goodall would serve as one of the most prominent faces, and consciences, of the animal welfare and conservation movement.

In typical fashion, Jane immediately took action. Her first efforts brought her to different countries in Africa where chimpanzees live. Meeting with presidents, government officials, and conservation organizations, Jane learned about the dangers faced by chimpanzees and the destruction of their native forests. As someone who had a great capacity to interact with all kinds of people, Jane now focused her attention on trying to convince government officials of the need to protect chimpanzees.

Jane's second goal was to improve conditions of the chimpanzees held in captivity for medical research. A large American biomedical research lab, Sema, Inc., housed some 500 primates in its facility. The lab had a high death rate, with accidents killing many chimps. The animals were placed in isolation in tiny cages, with barely enough room for them to move. While with her family during Christmas, Jane watched a videotape from the lab prepared by the watch group People for the Ethical Treatment of Animals (PETA) and was shattered. She and her family couldn't even speak after they had seen how the chimpanzees were treated.

So she went to see the lab at Sema herself, and she found the experience even more disturbing than she had anticipated. She saw chimps in solitary confinement, deprived of any stimulation. Jane picked up a small chimp and held her, giving her a piece of apple, but she hardly responded at all. Using what she had learned at

Jane visits chimpanzee Billy Jo at the Fauna Sanctuary, an animal retirement facility in Quebec, Canada. Billy Jo had been used in research for many years before being rescued.

Gombe, Jane told the scientists and lab technicians at Sema about the social organization of chimps, their emotional lives, and how they become depressed when isolated. She wrote, "The chimpanzees are more like us, genetically, than any other animal," but since they were not 100 percent human, "many laboratories were treating them like oversized rats." Would you, she asked, put a human child in a small cage alone with no companionship? Fortunately, the director of the lab listened and began to make changes to improve the lives of the chimps.

Jane then began to examine research centers worldwide. In Holland and in San Antonio, Texas, she found places where the physical environment was a bit better for chimps. Even more important, those who ran the facilities slowly made improvements.

"One day," she wrote, "perhaps quite soon, scientists may not need to use animals for testing drugs and for learning about human diseases ... But until that happens, it is desperately urgent that we try to give those animals being used today much better places to live, much better care, much more respect, and much more love."

Jane tickles a young chimp in the nursery, where chimpanzees went after being taken from their mothers, at New York University's Laboratory for Experimental Medicine and Surgery in Primates (LEMSIP). Many of the chimps were held in too-small cages, and Jane was saddened by what she saw. LEMSIP was shut down in 1997.

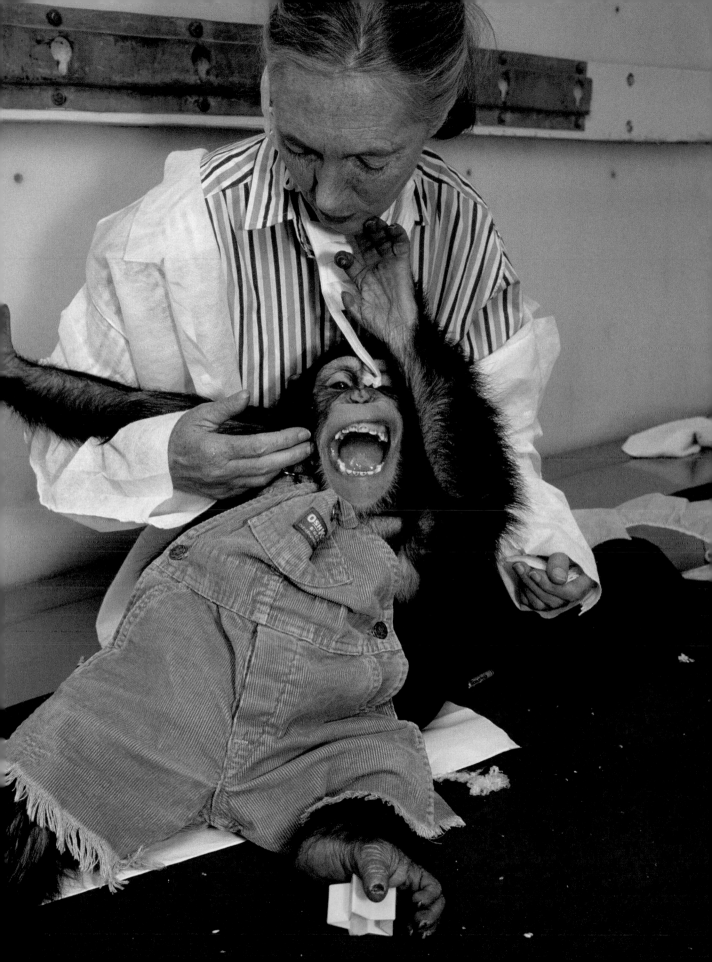

Rehabilitated Chimpanzees

In 2014, Jane Goodall turned 80. For her birthday she simply asked for money to return a group of rehabilitated chimps waiting in sanctuaries into the wild. In a powerful video, Jane explains her mission and shows the release of a chimpanzee called Wounda to a protected sanctuary on Tchindzoulou Island, in the Republic of the Congo. This battered, almost-dead chimp was brought back to life and then, finally, released.

Watch the video at janegoodall.org /media/videos /woundas-journey.

(Top) The Jane Goodall Institute Congo team transport chimpanzee Wounda on the Kouilou River to her release on Tchindzoulou Island.

(Above) Jane and the Tchimpounga Chimpanzee Rehabilitation Center's Rebeca Atencia release orphaned chimpanzee Wounda.

(Left) Wounda gives Jane a hug after her release.

Jane cares for a dehydrated chimp for sale on the streets of Kinshasa, Zaire (now the Democratic Republic of the Congo). The chimp was being sold for $300, but with the help of the American ambassador, Jane was able to rescue him.

As Jane visited different facilities, helping chimps in captivity, she found obstacles different from those at Gombe—but in many ways just as challenging. Many institutions treated chimps callously. Sometimes she started to cry when she was observing a chimp who had been mistreated. At one facility she saw a chimp in a tiny cage, and she began to weep. He reached out to touch her and then grabbed and bit off the tip of her right-hand thumb. Jane had to bear the pain of a hand she couldn't use for months, along with the memory of a facility that broke her heart.

Often her work brought her in contact with individual chimps whom she tried to help. She could not remain silent when she found even a single chimpanzee in trouble. One day at a tourist market in central Africa, Jane saw some chimpanzee babies for sale. One had a piece of cord tied around his waist and was placed on top of a tiny cage. His eyes were dull; he was curled up on his side. When she made chimpanzee greeting sounds, the baby sat up and touched her face.

Jane immediately called on the country's American ambassador, who contacted the country's minister of the environment. Although a law existed that made it illegal to sell chimps without a license, it was not being enforced. The police arrived at the site and

The Tchimpounga Chimpanzee Rehabilitation Center, which cares for orphaned chimpanzees, was created in 1992 through a partnership with the Jane Goodall Institute and the government of the Republic of the Congo. A caretaker at the sanctuary takes the youngest chimps into the nearby forest each day.

confiscated the infant, and Jane freed the chimp, cutting the rope with a knife. She then turned the sick infant over to a woman who cared for orphaned chimps and nurtured them back to health. Just as Jane made friends with chimps in Gombe, one animal at a time, she also saved captive and orphaned chimps, one at a time.

Slowly, one organization at a time, Jane helped secure better conditions for chimpanzees used in research all over the world. In 2013, the U.S. National Institutes of Health began retiring most of their research chimpanzees to sanctuaries. That same year a law was proposed in Congress to protect chimps in captivity under the Endangered Species Act. Never giving up, never discouraged, Jane has continued to press for better laboratory conditions and better laws all over the world.

Gregoire

Jane met one of her favorite chimps, Gregoire (pronounced "greg-warh"), while visiting a zoo in Congo. At that point, he was so thin that she could almost see every bone in his body. He lived alone in a black-floor cement cage. Born in 1942, Gregoire had endured these terrible conditions for 46 years. But he kept responding to humans. When a young girl approached the cage with a banana, she called to Gregoire and asked him to dance. Gregoire twirled around, drummed on a piece of furniture in the room, and then stood on his hands.

Jane couldn't stop thinking about Gregoire. What incredible strength had kept him alive? The Jane Goodall Institute secured better conditions for this old chimp and made sure he had some companions. Then, in May 1997, Gregoire and others from the zoo were moved to a rehabilitation center, where he lived for the rest of his life.

(Above) Gregoire displays his affection for Jane by grooming her hair.

(Below) After his rescue in the 1990s, Gregoire happily spent the rest of his life at the Jane Goodall Institute's Tchimpounga Chimpanzee Rehabilitation Center in southern Congo, where he had the company of young chimps.

Gregoire, who was first put in this cage in 1944, was Africa's oldest known chimpanzee at 66 years old, until his death in 2008.

Quite naturally, Jane also began to advocate for better treatment of chimps in zoos. Her research on the subject revealed that chimps were often held in cages that resembled prisons—with iron bars, concrete floors, and no socialization with others. So she launched project ChimpanZoo—an attempt to improve zoo conditions by environmental enrichment. The apes needed to be supplied with toys, bedding and nesting materials, fresh tree branches, and artificial termite mounds.

Having learned what stimulated chimps in the wild, Jane suggested ideal conditions for those in captivity. With project ChimpanZoo, Jane not only wanted to help chimps held in captivity; she also wanted to engage people in thinking about and caring for chimps. So, university professors and students could partner with zoo employees to determine how the behavior of chimps in captivity differed from the actions of those in

Gregoire snacks on yogurt at the Jane Goodall Institute's Tchimpounga Chimpanzee Rehabilitation Center. The center cares for more than 150 orphaned chimpanzees.

Jane plays with young chimps at New York University's Laboratory for Experimental Medicine and Surgery in Primates (LEMSIP). After LEMSIP was shut down, many of the chimps were rescued by sanctuaries.

the wild. These researchers could see how chimpanzee behavior differed depending on type of enclosure.

With the input of these researchers, over time conditions in many zoos began to change and more scientific information was collected and shared. And zoo administrators learned the value of enriching the lives of not only chimpanzees but other intelligent animals as well.

Chimp by chimp, Jane became involved in rescue missions around the world, always maintaining that "every individual matters." By holding research centers up to scrutiny, by arguing for good treatments in zoos, by finding sanctuaries for orphaned chimps, Jane fought to help protect captive and wild populations. As she said, "I spent years and years doing what I wanted to do most of all—being with wild, free chimpanzees in the forest. Now is my paying-back time."

Jane's Organizations

In 1977, Jane established the Jane Goodall Institute (JGI); today, JGI's three goals are to improve global understanding and treatment of great apes, to contribute to the preservation of the great ape species, and to create a worldwide network of young people (Roots & Shoots) who will care for all animals and the environment and take action on their behalf. In 1994, Jane founded the TACARE (Take Care) program to help people make good plans for their own communities.

Jane donates her lecture proceeds to JGI so that it can ensure funding for Roots & Shoots, studies at Gombe, and work around Africa.

Jane Goodall Institute

Jane established the Jane Goodall Institute for Research, Conservation, and Education in the United States to provide funds for research at Gombe. JGI has expanded since its founding to 27 other countries and now has two chimpanzee research centers at Congo's Tchimpounga sanctuary, where scientists study chimpanzees and topics such as human evolution, behavioral psychology, and geospatial mapping. JGI also takes on issues such as protecting great apes, improving local communities, and advocating for laws and public policy around the world.

Roots & Shoots

Roots & Shoots began in 1991 in Tanzania, where Jane was doing programs for schoolchildren. The group was called Roots & Shoots because roots move underground to make a firm foundation, and shoots, seeking the light, are initially weak but can eventually break down brick walls. With active chapters in more than 130 countries, members—from preschool through college—identify problems within their own area and work to improve conditions. Past projects include a German group that studied local wetlands; a chapter in China that worked to improve conditions for chimpanzees in the Shanghai zoo; and students in Oregon, U.S.A., who studied forest biodiversity. Jane writes to Roots & Shoots members all over the world, telling them to "Follow your dreams, work hard, and have FUN."

To find out more about Roots & Shoots, head to rootsandshoots.org.

TACARE

TACARE began with a team of dedicated Tanzanians working to improve the lives of people in villages—in ways suggested by the villagers themselves. Villagers can borrow small amounts of money to start their own environmentally sustainable projects—like a tree nursery. JGI and the local people have also become partners in conservation. Trained forest monitors use smartphones and tablets to record every time they see an illegally cut tree, cartridges from a gun, a trap, or a fire. JGI operates similar programs around chimpanzee habitats in four other countries: Uganda, the Democratic Republic of the Congo, the Republic of the Congo, and Senegal.

Because of the work of TACARE, Gombe's chimps have three times more forest than they had in 1991.

"Every individual matters. Every individual has a role to play. Every individual makes a difference."
—JANE GOODALL

THE LEGACY

Making the World a Better Place for Animals

Because Jane Goodall risked her life again and again in the wild to study chimpanzees, 50 years later the field of chimpanzee research looks completely different. Jane showed the world that our nearest ancestors were worth observing and understanding.

But in 50 years a great deal has changed in terms of what we know about chimpanzees and how they can be studied. Some of that research certainly looks a great deal tamer than anything Jane did in her first years at Gombe. Today, scientists understand that chimps can do more than forage for termites

Jane with LaVieille and her new little friend at the Tchimpounga Chimpanzee Rehabilitation Center in the Republic of the Congo

Congo, the London Zoo's artistic chimpanzee, at work on his new masterpiece in 1957. Three of Congo's paintings were sold at an art auction in 2005 for £14,400 ($26,248)—20 times their original estimate. Famous artist Pablo Picasso even owned one of Congo's 400 works.

with tools. Chimps can solve problems and plan ahead. Captive chimps have learned as many as 350 signs in American Sign Language (ASL). Chimps have also produced drawings and paintings, which, on occasion, have sold for thousands of dollars at auctions.

Zoologist Desmond Morris first observed a chimp, Congo, who learned how to create art. At age two, Congo began to draw, and by four he had made more than 200 abstract compositions. Congo mastered circles; he balanced compositions on each side of the page; he painted in a fan pattern. And he even threw artistic temper tantrums if his creation was taken away too soon.

Using Sign Language

Born in Africa around September 1965, Washoe (pronounced "wa-show") was believed to have been captured and sold in a market. When Drs. Allen and Beatrix Gardner adopted her from military scientists at ten months old, she was named for the county where they lived in Nevada, U.S.A. Slowly they taught Washoe American Sign Language, and one day she signed "water" and "bird" upon seeing a swan.

Washoe eventually lived at both the University of Oklahoma and Central Washington University. Her favorite foods were oatmeal with onions, pumpkin pudding, split pea soup, and eggplant. She loved looking through books, magazines, and catalogs, and she was particularly taken with shoe catalogs. In fact, Washoe always checked out the footwear of her human companions. If she spotted new shoes, she would sign to have them shown to her!

Washoe taught American Sign Language to her adopted son, Loulis. Both are shown in this photograph in Norman, Oklahoma, U.S.A., on October 22, 1979.

This chimpanzee at the Ngamba Island Chimpanzee Sanctuary, in Uganda, shows off some intricate tool use to extract honey from a hole in an artificial termite mound.

Research on chimp creativity has continued over the years. In 2013, the Humane Society of the United States ran an art contest for chimpanzees in sanctuaries, which Jane helped judge—"All of the art was beautiful and unique—just like chimpanzees," she said. A 37-year-old chimpanzee who lives in Chimp Haven, in Louisiana, U.S.A., won the contest. Instead of using his humanlike hands, he paints with his tongue, and his winning composition was created in bright colors of blue, violet, yellow, and turquoise.

Jane observed that chimpanzees used gestures and expressions to communicate in the wild. But they can even replicate human sign language. Washoe, a female chimp, became the first to communicate in ASL. She learned around 350 words and actually taught some signs to another chimp, Loulis. In 1967, psychologists Allen and Beatrix Gardner began teaching Washoe sign language at the University of Nevada, Reno, in the United States. They treated her like one of the family, dressing her up in clothes and including her at the table for dinner. Washoe had her own trailer where she lived, did chores, played outdoors, and even took rides in the car.

Advances in technology have made it possible for scientists to study chimpanzees by using easier methods than Jane ever had at her disposal. She needed to do all her work with binoculars, a pen, and a pad of paper. Now field researchers carry laptop computers to record data quickly and they use radio collars to follow chimps being rereleased into the wild. Satellite imagery allows scientists to measure accurately the habitat of chimps and the changes over time. With geographic information systems (GIS) software scientists can map chimp activities and the natural resources in the area. Showing single trees and buildings, the software alerts researchers to human threats to the habitat of chimps—such as settlements and farms. High-resolution satellite images show details of areas that are remote or inaccessible by land. Even the casual researcher can obtain information once hard to come by using many Internet tools. While sitting at home, an interested person can now take a flight over Gombe while reading blog entries from those working there.

Jane, no longer able to spend much time at Gombe because of her globe-trotting conservation efforts, still finds great joy in watching the Gombe chimps when she does return to the park.

Jane's Tips for Kids Who Want to Work With Animals

1 Watch animals and see what they do.

2 Keep a notebook and write down observations.

3 Come up with ideas about why animals are behaving the way they are.

4 Find out how they are doing their daily activities.

5 Make a map of where they travel.

6 Go on nature walks.

7 Watch the way a caterpillar pupates and emerges as a butterfly.

8 Observe birds making nests.

9 Pay attention to family pets and learn from them.

10 Do not frighten or hurt animals and speak up if you see someone doing so.

As a researcher, Jane spent countless hours hidden in the vegetation, observing the chimps through binoculars.

Some of the scientific breakthroughs in the past 50 years have dramatically changed how animals can be studied and what can be learned from them. One of the best ways to research animals in the wild, and not disturb them, is to study their excrement and urine. Often, new students going into remote areas to study animals begin their work by collecting feces! In Gombe, Jane would often dissolve chimpanzee dung in water to find out what the animals had eaten. But after breakthroughs in DNA analysis, scientists discovered that every animal's poop has a unique DNA.

Jane, Hugo, and their son, Grub, watch and film baboons in Tanzania, in this photograph from 1976.

That means that just by gathering scat in an area, researchers can tell how many animals are living there and what bacteria or viruses those animals have. Scientists have even analyzed fossilized dinosaur poop to discover the grasses the dinosaurs ate. By studying chimpanzee scat from western Africa, scientists found a virus SIVcpz, the precursor to the human virus HIV, which can lead to AIDS.

DNA research on chimps stands at the cutting edge of science. With more and more sophisticated technology being developed to study the difference of one DNA strain from another, scientists have been debating how similar chimpanzees are to humans.

In 2005, a study by 67 researchers from the Chimp Sequencing and Analysis Consortium analyzed how close chimpanzee and human blood were in terms of DNA. Their findings suggest that the DNA of chimps and humans differs by only 1.01 to 4 percent. Although scientists disagree on the precise number, all agree that chimpanzees and bonobos are more similar to humans than any other living creature.

An African forest elephant walks along a beach. This photograph, by National Geographic photographer Michael Nichols, was taken with a camera trap.

When Jane wanted to understand which chimps were related, she had to spend long hours observing who traveled together and interacted with one another. DNA analysis allows scientists to easily determine a chimp's family members, since chimps inherit their DNA from their parents. Jane and other early researchers painstakingly developed charts of the Gombe chimp families. Today such family charts can be drawn up simply by DNA analysis.

Another area of breakthroughs has come in the changing technologies of photography. Veteran cameraman Michael Nichols, who has traveled with Jane in the field many times, has said he wishes he were starting out today as a photographer. Earlier photographers had to use a tripod, which was heavy and hard to carry.

New Technology for Photographing Wild Animals

A remotely activated digital camera, or camera trap, usually has a motion sensor and an infrared flash and will take photos day or night. It can be placed in the ground, in trees, or on steel poles. These cameras capture animals on film and make it possible for a great deal of scientific data to be gathered with little human interference. After being secured, the camera trap operates continuously; unlike human field researchers, it does not need rest or sleep.

Camera traps not only allow the monitoring of a known animal population but also have documented many rare or endangered species. Several organizations such as the BBC and the National Geographic Society conduct photographic contests for the most visually exciting images recorded by camera traps.

(Above) By photographing chimpanzees with camera traps, researchers in Congo's Nouabalé-Ndoki National Park have been able to observe behaviors never before seen by humans.

(Below) Researchers set up controller camera traps near an ant nest to observe the ants' behavior.

This touching moment for Jane came when Jou Jou, a full-grown male chimpanzee, reached out his hand to Jane in greeting. He had been caged for years in Congo's Brazzaville Zoo; a social animal, he was desperate for contact with other living beings.

Camera traps, remotely activated cameras, are equipped with a motion sensor or an infrared sensor. They allow researchers to capture wild animals on film without actually being present. And the data can be sent anywhere in the world to be reviewed at any point in time. Best of all, camera traps do not disturb or interfere with the wildlife in an area being observed. As Nichols has said, "Chimpanzees are incredibly hard to follow. They can move silently ... Gombe is one of the toughest places on Earth to follow chimps. That doesn't change. But the techniques are far easier. In the Congo, I did a lot of work with camera traps. You still have to go out into the terrain, but you don't have to carry a tripod."

Camera traps also make it possible to record chimp activity for hours at a time. Chimps in one area groom one way; chimps in another area groom another way. They develop their own local customs. Because scientists can watch hours of chimp activity, they can observe slight variations in chimpanzee behavior in different locations.

The young scientists going into the field today have new technologies, new methods, and new computer programs at their disposal. These advancements allow scientists today to study chimpanzees with great precision.

For more than 50 years, chimpanzees and our relationship to these animals have been the focus of Jane Goodall's work. As a child, Jane knew that she wanted to go to Africa and be with wild animals. After she accomplished that dream, she used her fame to fight for animals on Earth.

Jane believes that anyone who loves animals can take that passion and turn it into a path for life. All animals matter. All life matters. And our planet can be changed by one small action at a time, by helping one animal at a time. As Jane has said, "Together we can make the world a better place for all living things."

A chimpanzee mother holds her baby close in Gombe National Park. In the wild, a chimpanzee will usually give birth to one baby every five or six years. The young chimp may stay with his or her mother for about seven years.

The Lives She Touches

For more than 50 years, Jane Goodall has inspired people around the globe, young and old, to take action to save the environment and to protect animals. Thousands of testimonies about her have been given over the years. Here are six typical stories, two from people she worked closely with, four from children whose lives she changed.

Mary Smith

As a young photography editor for *National Geographic,* Mary first met Jane Goodall in 1962 on a street in Nairobi, Kenya. Mary, who also worked with Louis Leakey, has been able to observe Jane Goodall for more than 50 years and considers her the "most impressive person I know. Her focus has been extraordinary; she always seems to know what the next five steps are. She seizes every

opportunity to promote those things that are important to her. She spends nothing on herself. She lives a life not about herself. Her actions are the actions of a true believer; she has totally devoted herself to her cause."

MADISON and RHIANNON

Madison (left) and Rhiannon (right) joined Roots & Shoots when they were seventh graders. They decided to raise awareness of the endangered orangutan to earn a Girl Scout Bronze Award. They founded Project ORANGS (projectorangs.org) to bring attention to the environmental impact of unsustainable palm oil, an ingredient of many products, including Girl Scout cookies.

Michael Nichols

Called the Indiana Jones of photography, Michael Nichols began working with Jane Goodall in the late 1980s on a variety of articles and a book, *Brutal Kinship*. He says, "Jane Goodall is gentle but firm. She's a role model for so many women on the planet. She's an animal lover but also a scientist. She's able to walk with presidents and with the poorest people on Earth. She needs nothing. She is very austere. She has all the qualities that people should respect. She's never stopped; she's stayed true to her mission and works harder today than she did when she was a field-worker with chimpanzees. She is completely genuine—exactly the person the world thinks she is."

MARIAH

In third grade, Mariah was inspired by Jane Goodall's devotion to making a positive impact on a single community. Mariah started a summer reading program at Bole Community School in Addis Ababa, Ethiopia, to fight illiteracy through the use of e-readers.

ANTHONY

Anthony heard about Jane Goodall in high school. He wanted to spread her message to his community as the United Nations Messenger of Peace. He began pursuing a project aimed at stopping school violence via an anti-bullying petition. This petition was introduced into the New York City Council through his efforts.

GENEVIEVE

Genevieve joined Roots & Shoots in elementary school, when she actually met Jane and became involved in a local animal shelter. Now in high school, Genevieve has started a group that brings teens into the shelter to provide love and nurturing to the animals.

FIELD NOTES
Resources and More

All About Chimpanzees

1   The chimpanzee's scientific name is *Pan troglodytes*.

2   Humans and chimpanzees share 95 to 98 percent of the same DNA.

3   Chimpanzees are now endangered, with only 170,000 to 300,000 alive in the world.

4   Chimpanzees live in 21 countries in Africa. Most live in the rain forests, which are being cut down.

5   Chimpanzees forage for food six to eight hours a day.

6   Chimpanzees live in social groups or communities.

7   Chimpanzees sleep in trees, using nests of leafy branches.

8   Chimpanzees clean themselves by wiping mud or blood off with leaves.

9   Young chimps learn from observing their mothers or other adults. If a mother chimpanzee dies, her offspring might be adopted by an older brother, sister, or even an unrelated adult.

10   Chimpanzees in the wild rarely live longer than 50 years.

Baby chimps cling to the fur on their mother's belly as she walks. Later they ride on her back until about the age of five, or until the next infant is born.

Chimpanzees walk using their arms and legs. They use their knuckles for support and are thus called "knuckle walkers."

The chimpanzees of Gombe weigh between 90 and 115 pounds (41 and 52 kg). In other parts of West Africa, they might be even larger; female chimps are smaller.

Chimpanzees are omnivores, eating mainly fruits, nuts, seeds, blossoms, leaves, eggs, and insects. But they will kill and eat small animals.

Chimpanzees have opposable thumbs and big toes—so they can grip objects with their feet.

When chimpanzees are frightened, their hair stands on end.

Frodo

Known for his size, strength, and aggression, Frodo ruled as alpha male at Gombe for about five years. He liked to frighten animals and humans and one time even attacked Jane. But once out of power, he changed and became more peaceful.

Gizmo

A small playful chimp, Gizmo ran around his brothers and sisters, looking for a hug or to play. His mother, Gremlin, weaned him early, and Gizmo became needy for attention from his family.

Samwise

Named for the hobbit Sam in J. R. R. Tolkien's books, Sam at age 12 is still close to her mother. But when she is ready to breed, Sam will have to decide whether to stay at Gombe or leave the family and go to another area to avoid mating with family members. About half of the females of Gombe leave their home for another in adolescence.

Gaia

A nurturing chimp, Gaia is a member of what Jane termed the "G family." Her mother, Gremlin, took three of Gaia's infants to try to raise them. Despite this, Gaia stayed close to the family when they traveled or fished for termites. She helped raise her mother's twins, Golden and Glitter, the only Gombe chimp twins to survive to adulthood. After her mother died, Gaia had baby Google in 2009.

Gombe Family Scrapbook

Sparrow With Children and Grandchildren

Here Sparrow, at age 54, enjoys a grooming session with extended members of the S family. Sparrow was known for raising very strong and competent daughters—but her sons were "mama's boys."

Mr. Worzle

Mr. Worzle had a best friend, Leakey, who he traveled with all the time. Leakey was a robust, high-ranking chimpanzee, while Mr. Worzle was nervous and low ranking. But the two spent hours together, feeding, building their nests in the same place, and grooming each other.

Figan

Jane connected with Figan, whom she considered especially intelligent, when he was a young chimp. He was always intrigued by the power structure of the males at Gombe and used his affiliation with his brother Fagan to eventually become the alpha male of the group.

Nasa

Every now and then an immigrant chimp arrived in Gombe; in 2000 Nasa showed up. Her name comes from the Swahili word meaning "to grasp." A large chimp, she mainly hung out with females. But the young adult males often included this strong chimp on their patrols.

The Life of Jane Goodall: A Time Line

April 3, 1934
Valerie Jane Morris-Goodall is born in London.

Fall 1939
Jane hides for hours in a henhouse to discover how chickens lay eggs.

1952
Jane graduates from high school.

April 1957
Jane travels to Kenya to visit her friend Clo Mange.

July 1960
Jane begins her work at Gombe Stream Game Reserve, accompanied by her mother, Vanne.

1962
Jane enters the University of Cambridge as a Ph.D. candidate.

1962 & 1964
Jane receives the Franklin Burr Award from NGS for her contribution to science.

August 1963
"My Life Among Wild Chimpanzees" appears in *National Geographic*.

March 1964
Jane marries Hugo van Lawick.

Summer 1964
Jane sees chimpanzees using leaves to clean themselves and chewing leaves to use as sponges to soak up water.

March 1967
Jane's son, Hugo Eric Louis van Lawick, nicknamed Grub, is born.

1971
Jane's autobiography *In the Shadow of Man* is published and becomes a best seller.

1974
Jane and Hugo van Lawick divorce.

1975
Jane marries her second husband, Hon. Derek Bryceson, director of Tanzanian national parks.

1977
The Jane Goodall Institute is established.

1990
Jane receives the Kyoto Prize in basic science from Japan.

February 1991
Jane founds Roots & Shoots.

1995
Jane receives NGS's Hubbard Medal.

1999
Jane's eighth book, *Reason for Hope*, becomes a *New York Times* best seller.

2001
Jane is awarded the Gandhi-King Award for Non-Violence.

October 1960
Jane observes chimpanzees eating meat.

November 1960
Jane sees chimp David Greybeard using tools.

January 1961
Jane first sees chimpanzees performing a "rain dance."

March 1961
Jane receives a grant from the National Geographic Society's (NGS) Committee for Research and Exploration.

1967
Gombe Stream Game Reserve becomes Gombe National Park.

1966
Chimps are afflicted with polio.

December 1965
Miss Goodall and the Wild Chimpanzees appears on television.

1965
Jane receives her Ph.D. from Cambridge, becoming the eighth person to get a Ph.D. without first getting an undergraduate degree.

1965
The Gombe Stream Research Center is founded.

May 1979
Jane presents new Gombe findings in "Life and Death at Gombe" in *National Geographic*.

1980
Jane's husband, Derek, passes away after a battle with cancer.

1984
Jane's second National Geographic special, *Jane Goodall: Among the Wild Chimpanzees*, airs.

1984
ChimpanZoo project begins.

November 1986
The Chicago, U.S.A., conference that transforms Jane's mission takes place.

2003
Jane receives the Benjamin Franklin Medal in Life Science.

2004
Jane is made a Dame of the British Empire.

2008
Jane receives the French Legion of Honor award and a UNESCO Gold Medal.

2010
Film *Jane's Journey* opens.

2014
Jane celebrates her 80th birthday. ❖

Map of Gombe

Wild chimpanzees are found only in Africa. Jane's focus area was in the easternmost part of their range, within Tanzania.

A F R I C A

Western Chimpanzee

Nigerian Chimpanzee

Eastern Chimpanzee

Central African Chimpanzee

Bonobo

TANZANIA

Ranges of Chimpanzee Subspecies

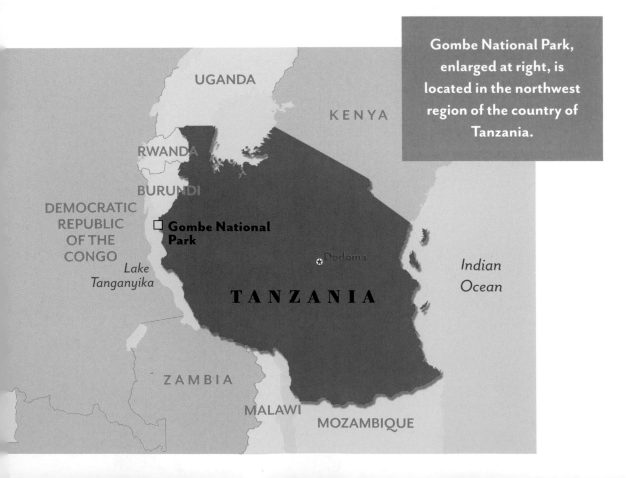

Gombe National Park, enlarged at right, is located in the northwest region of the country of Tanzania.

UGANDA

KENYA

RWANDA

BURUNDI

DEMOCRATIC REPUBLIC OF THE CONGO

□ **Gombe National Park**

Lake Tanganyika

Dodoma

Indian Ocean

T A N Z A N I A

ZAMBIA

MALAWI

MOZAMBIQUE

Mwamgongo

Miles
0   1.5

0   1.5
Kilometers

Map Key

Road

Trail

Buildings

Forest

Park boundary

Lake Tanganyika

Kichwa cha
Fisi Mt.

Linda
Peak

Jane's
Peak

**Gombe Stream
Research Center**

Rocky
Peak

Kakombe Valley

Milenda
Kibanda Mt.

Msekela Hills

Nondwa Hill

Mgonya

Milundi Mt.

Chankele

Mgazi

Bubango Hill

Bubango

Mvezi

Karakihuma
Mt.

Kabulanzwila
Hill

Kilembela

*Rasi
Kazinga*

Kitunda Mt.

Bitale

Kazinga

Find Out More

BOOKS

De la Bédoyère, Camilla. *No One Loved Gorillas More: Dian Fossey: Letters From the Mist.* Washington, D.C.: National Geographic, 2005.

McDonnell, Patrick. *Me ... Jane.* New York: Little Brown, 2011.

Montgomery, Sy. *Walking With the Great Apes: Jane Goodall, Dian Fossey, Biruté Galdikas.* New York: Houghton Mifflin, 1991.

Nichols, Michael, Jane Goodall, George B. **Schaller, and Mary G. Smith.** *The Great Apes: Between Two Worlds.* Washington, D.C.: National Geographic, 1993.

Ottaviani, Jim, and Maris Wicks. *Primates: The Fearless Science of Jane Goodall, Dian Fossey, and Biruté Galdikas.* New York: First Second, 2013.

Peterson, Dale. *Jane Goodall: The Woman Who Redefined Man.* New York: Mariner Books, 2008.

Winter, Jeanette. *The Watcher: Jane Goodall's Life With the Chimps.* New York: Schwartz & Wade, 2011.

BOOKS BY JANE GOODALL

For Young Readers

The Chimpanzee Family Book. New York: North-South Books, 1989.

The Chimpanzees I Love: Saving Their World and Ours. New York: Scholastic, 2001.

Dr. White. New York: North-South Books, 1999.

The Eagle and the Wren. New York: North-South Books, 2000.

Grub: The Bush Baby. Boston: Houghton Mifflin, 1972.

My Life With the Chimpanzees: The Fascinating Story of One of the World's Most Celebrated Naturalists. New York: Simon & Schuster, 1988.

Rickie and Henri: A True Story. New York: Minedition, 2004.

With Love: Ten Heartwarming Stories of Chimpanzees in the Wild. New York: North-South Books, 1994.

For Older Readers

Africa in My Blood: An Autobiography in Letters. Vol. 1, *The Early Years.* Edited by Dale Peterson. Boston: Houghton Mifflin, 2000.

Beyond Innocence: An Autobiography in Letters. Vol. 2, *The Later Years.* Edited by Dale Peterson. Boston: Houghton Mifflin, 2001.

Brutal Kinship (with Michael Nichols). New York: Aperture Foundation, 1999.

The Chimpanzees of Gombe: Patterns of Behavior. Boston: Belknap Press, 1986.

Jane Goodall: 40 Years at Gombe. New York: Stewart, Tabori & Chang, 2000.

Jane Goodall: 50 Years at Gombe. New York: Stewart, Tabori & Chang, 2010.

Harvest for Hope: A Guide to Mindful Eating (with Gary McAvoy and Gail Hudson). New York: Warner Books, 2005.

Hope for Animals and Their World: How Endangered Species Are Being Rescued From the Brink (with Thane Maynard and Gail Hudson). New York: Grand Central Publishing, 2009.

In the Shadow of Man. Boston: Houghton Mifflin, 1971.

Innocent Killers (with Hugo van Lawick). Boston: Houghton Mifflin, 1971.

My Friends the Wild Chimpanzees. Washington, D.C.: National Geographic, 1969.

Solo: The Story of an African Wild (with Hugo van Lawick). Boston: Houghton Mifflin, 1974.

Through a Window: My Thirty Years With the Chimpanzees of Gombe. Boston: Houghton Mifflin, 1990.

Visions of Caliban: On Chimpanzees and People (with Dale Peterson). Athens: University of Georgia Press, 1991.

Reason for Hope: A Spiritual Journey (with Phillip Berman). New York: Grand Central Publishing, 1999.

Seeds of Hope: Wisdom and Wonder From the World of Plants (with Gail Hudson). New York: Grand Central Publishing, 2014.

The Ten Trusts: What We Must Do to Care for the Animals We Love (with Marc Bekoff). New York: HarperCollins, 2002.

FILMS

Chimpanzee. Disney Nature, 2013.

Chimps: So Like Us. HBO, 1990.

Jane. Washington, D.C.: National Geographic, 2014.

Jane Goodall: Among the Wild Chimpanzees. Washington, D.C.: National Geographic, 1984.

Jane Goodall: My Life With Chimpanzees. Washington, D.C.: National Geographic, 2009.

Jane Goodall's Wild Chimpanzees. IMAX, 2002.

Jane's Journey. First Run Features, 2010.

Notes

Chapter 1: Childhood

10 "If you really want something ..." Dale Peterson, *Jane Goodall*, 58.

13 "hairless from all the loving" Jane Goodall, *Reason for Hope*, 5.

15 "I can see, with almost unbearable clarity ..." Jane Goodall, *Reason for Hope*, 276–277.

18 "I was never, ever told ..." Dale Peterson, *Jane Goodall*, 29–30.

18 "dreary," "routine and dullness," "stuffed with 'education' ..." Dale Peterson, *Jane Goodall*, 56–57.

21 "earning a living ... almost frightening" Dale Peterson, *Jane Goodall*, 69.

21 "boredom of this foul job" Dale Peterson, *Jane Goodall*, 76.

22 "idyllic" Jane Goodall and Gail Hudson, *Seeds of Hope*, chapter 1, excerpted on website of *Here & Now*, an NPR radio news program produced at WBUR, with the transcript of "Jane Goodall Plants 'Seeds of Hope'," April 17, 2014, http://hereandnow.wbur.org/2014/04/17/goodall-seeds-hope.

Chapter 2: Gombe

24 "One of the males ..." Jane Goodall, "My Life Among Wild Chimpanzees," *National Geographic*, August 1983, 274.

24 "Right from the moment ..." Dale Peterson, *Jane Goodall*, 92.

26 "uncluttered by theories" Jane Goodall, *My Life With the Chimpanzees*, 48.

26 "Louis, I wish ..." Dale Peterson, *Jane Goodall*, 117.

26 "I've been waiting ..." Jane Goodall, *My Life With the Chimpanzees*, 48.

29 "It is so beautiful ..." Dale Peterson, *Jane Goodall*, 179.

31 "an ingrained illogical fear" Jane Goodall, *In the Shadow of Man*, 31.

34 "dreamed of seeing anything so exciting" Jane Goodall, *In the Shadow of Man*, 35.

34 "Now we must ..." Dale Peterson, *Jane Goodall*, 212.

36 "the sweetest little thing" Dale Peterson, *Jane Goodall*, 137.

Chapter 3: Celebrity Scientist

38 "It is so beautiful ..." Dale Peterson, *Jane Goodall*, 179.

46 "chimp—chimp—and more chimp ..." Dale Peterson, *Jane Goodall*, 327.

48 "paradise" Dale Peterson, *Jane Goodall*, 180.

Chapter 4: Transformation

52 "Now I want to share " Jane Goodall, *My Life With the Chimpanzees*, 105.

52 "When I arrived at Chicago ..." Dale Peterson, *Jane Goodall*, 601.

55 "This is no time ..." Joseph Loconte, "Winston Churchill's July 4 Message to America," *Weekly Standard* (blog), July 4, 2010, http://www.weeklystandard.com/blogs/winston-churchill's-july-4-message-america.

56 "The chimpanzees are more like us ..." Jane Goodall, *Beyond Innocence*, 318.

56 "One day, perhaps quite soon ..." Jane Goodall, *My Life With the Chimpanzees*, 134–135.

63 "every individual matters" Jane Goodall, *Reason for Hope*, 297.

63 "I spent years and years ..." Jane Goodall, *My Life With the Chimpanzees*, 146.

65 "Follow your dreams ..." Jane Goodall, *Beyond Innocence*, 396.

Chapter 5: The Legacy

66 "Every individual matters ..." Jane Goodall, *Reason for Hope*, 297.

70 "All of the art ..." Harriet Gibsone, "Chimpanzee Wins $10,000 Prize for Abstract Painting," *Guardian*, August 30, 2013, http://www.theguardian.com/artanddesign/2013/aug/30/chimpanzee-wins-10000-dollars-abstract-painting.

76 "Chimpanzees are incredibly hard ..." Michael Nichols (editor at large, wildlife photographer, *National Geographic*) in discussion with the author, January 3, 2014.

77 "Together we can make ..." Jane Goodall, *My Life With the Chimpanzees*, 156.

78 "most impressive person ..." Mary Smith (former *National Geographic* senior editor) in discussion with the author, January 10, 2014.

79 "Jane Goodall is gentle ..." Michael Nichols (editor at large, wildlife photographer, *National Geographic*) in discussion with the author, January 3, 2014.

84 Gombe Family Scrapbook adapted from "Gombe Family Album," *National Geographic*, August 2014, 52–65.

Index

Index and Photo Credits

PHOTO CREDITS

NGC: National Geographic Creative; JGI: The Jane Goodall Institute

Plant Illustrations by Susan Crawford

Cover: (Jane Goodall), CBS/Landov; (baby chimp), Gerry Ellis/Minden Pictures; Spine, Gerry Ellis/Minden Pictures; Back Cover (Jane Goodall and chimp), Derek N. Bryceson/NGC; Back Flap, courtesy Anita Silvey; Trade case, Antony Souter/Alamy; 1, Michael Nichols/NGC; 2–3, Michael Nichols/NGC; 5, Craig Packer/NGC; 6, Hugo van Lawick/NGC; 8 (LE), courtesy JGI; 8 (RT), Michael Nichols/NGC; 9, Shutterstock; 10–11, courtesy JGI; 12, the Goodall family, courtesy JGI; 13, Michael Nichols/NGC; 14, courtesy JGI; 15 (INSET), Ivan Van Laningham; 15 (BACK), Kristin J. Mosher; 16, courtesy JGI; 17, SSPL/NRM/Pictorial Collection/Getty Images; 18, the Goodall family, courtesy JGI; 19, courtesy JGI; 19 (BACK), Helen Hotson/Alamy; 20, the Goodall family, courtesy JGI; 20 (BACK), Kristin J Mosher; 22, postcard courtesy Alwyn Ladell/Flickr.com; 22–23 (BACK), Helen Hotson/Alamy; 23 (UP), Hulton Archive/Getty Images; 23 (LO), Marco Regalia/Alamy; 24–25, Hugo van Lawick/NGC; 26, Antony Souter/Alamy; 27 (UP), Robert F. Sisson/NGC; 27, Anup Shah/naturepl.com; 28 (RT), Hugo van Lawick, courtesy JGI; 28 (LE), Anup Shah/naturepl.com; 29, Judy Goodall, courtesy JGI; 30, Hugo van Lawick/NGC; 31 (RT), Rod Williams/naturepl.com; 31 (BACK), Kristin J. Mosher; 32, Michael Nichols/NGC; 33, Hugo van Lawick/NGC; 33 (BACK), Gerry Ellis/Minden Pictures; 34–35 (LO), courtesy JGI; 35 (UP), Hugo van Lawick/NGC; 35 (LO), courtesy JGI; 36–37 (BACK), Kristin J. Mosher; 36 (UP), Tim Fitzharris/Minden Pictures; 36 (LO), Cynictis Penicillata/naturepl.com; 37 (UP), Gerry Ellis/Minden Pictures; 37 (CTR), Shin Yoshino/Minden Pictures; 37 (LO), Richard Du Toit/Minden Pictures; 38–39, Hugo van Lawick/NGC; 40, Hugo van Lawick/NGC; 41 (RT), Hugo van Lawick, courtesy JGI; 41 (BACK), Anup Shah/naturepl.com; 42, Joan Travis, courtesy JGI; 43, courtesy JGI; 44 (UP), Cyril Ruoso/JH Editorial/Minden Pictures/NGC; 44 (CTR), Ingo Arndt/Minden Pictures/Minden Pictures; 44 (LO), Antony Souter/Alamy; 44 (BACK), Anup Shah/naturepl.com; 45, Vanne Goodall, courtesy JGI; 46 (ALL), Kodachromes by Baron Hugo van Lawick, National Geographic Magazine; 47, Jane Goodall; 47 (BACK), Kristin J. Mosher; 48, Hugo van Lawick, courtesy JGI; 49, Mike Quan/NGC; 50–51 (BACK), Kristin J. Mosher; 50 (LE), Ektachrome by Robert M. Campbell © NGS National Geographic Magazine; 50 (RT), Robert I.M. Campbell/NGC; 51 (LE), Rodney Brindamour/NGC; 51 (RT), photography by Rod Brindamour, National Geographic Magazine; 52–53, Michael Nichols/NGC; 54 (UP), Michael Nichols/NGC; 54 (LO), Michael Nichols/NGC; 56, Fauna Sanctuary/New England Anti-Vivisection Society; 57, Michael Nichols/NGC; 58 (UPRT), Michael Cox, courtesy JGI; 58 (LOLE), Michael Cox, courtesy JGI; 58 (LORT), Michael Cox, courtesy JGI; 58 (BACK), Gerry Ellis/Minden Pictures; 59, Michael Nichols/NGC; 60, Michael Nichols/NGC; 61 (UPRT), Michael Nichols/NGC; 61 (LOLE), Michael Nichols/NGC; 61 (LORT), Michael Nichols/NGC; 61 (BACK), Kristin J. Moshi; 62, Fernando Turmo, courtesy JGI; 63, Michael Nichols/NGC; 64–65 (BACK), Gerry Ellis/Minden Pictures; 64 (UP), Jane Goodall Institute-UK, courtesy JGI; 64 (LO), Bill Wallauer, courtesy JGI; 65 (UP), Chris Dickinson, courtesy JGI; 65 (LO), courtesy JGI; 66–67, Fernando Turmo, courtesy JGI; 68, William Vanderson/Hulton Archives/Getty Images; 69, AP Images; 69 (BACK), Kristin J. Mosher; 70, Suzi Eszterhas/Minden Pictures; 71, Michael Nichols/NGC; 72, Hugo van Lawick, courtesy JGI; 72 (BACK), Anup Shah/naturepl.com; 73, Everett Collection Inc./Alamy; 74, Michael Nichols/NGC; 75 (UP), Ian Nichols/NGC; 75 (LO), Ian Nichols/NGC; 75 (BACK), Kristin J. Mosher; 76, Michael Nichols/NGC; 77, Gerry Ellis/Minden Pictures; 78–79 (BACK), Kristin J. Mosher; 78 (UP), courtesy Mary Smith; 78 (LO), courtesy JGI; 79 (UP), Michael Nichols/NGC; 79 (UP), Roy Toft/NGC; 79 (LO LE, LO CTR), courtesy JGI; 79 (LO RT), Emily Rhodes/Jane Goodall's Roots & Shoots; 80–81, Hugo van Lawick/NGC; 82 (LE), Anup Shah/naturepl.com; 82 (RT), Eric Isselee/Shutterstock; 83, Eric Isselee/Shutterstock; 84 (ALL CHIMPS), Fiona Rogers/www.shahrogersphoto.com/NGC; 84 (BACK), Shutterstock; 85 (UP), Fiona Rogers/www.shahrogersphoto.com/NGC; 85 (LO), Fiona Rogers/www.shahrogersphoto.com/NGC; 86 (ALL), Anup Shah/www.shahrogersphotogr.com/NGC; 87 (UP), courtesy JGI; 87 (LO), Fiona Rogers/www.shahrogersphoto.com/NGC; 88–89 (BACK), Kristin J MosherImages Images; 90 (BACK), Shutterstock

-LYNNFIELD PUBLIC LIBRARY-
LYNNFIELD, MA 01940